鎌倉佐弓句集

薔薇かんむり

Sayumi Kamakura

Haiku Collection

A Crown of Roses

英訳　ジェームス・シェイ　ジム・ケイシャン

English translations by James Shea & Jim Kacian

2016

First Edition: 2007, Second Edition: 2009
Third Edition: 2009, Fourth Edition 2016
Rs. 150/-

Cyberwit.net
HIG 45 Kaushambi Kunj, Kalindipuram
Allahabad - 211011 (U.P.) India
http://www.cyberwit.net
Tel: +(91) 9415091004 +(91) (532) 2552257
E-mail: info@cyberwit.net

Printed at Repro India Limited.

Foreword

The American poet James Wright once cited the power of the word "actually" in Robert Frost's short poem "Lodged," saying "that one adverb, it seems to me, strikes like a bullet." Haiku, in particular, puts tremendous pressure on every word, and Sayumi Kamakura's poems typically hinge on one word, reverberating through the line, as in the verb "shigamitsuku" or "cling" in the following:

夏の果スポンジに水しがみつく
Natsu no hate suponji ni mizu shigamitsuku

The end of summer—

water clings

to a sponge

Kamakura also has a knack for conveying a joyous burst of energy, revealing her gift for surprising the reader with a couple of syllables:

ポストまで歩けば二分走れば春
posuto made arukeba nibun hashireba haru

Walking, it's two minutes

to the mailbox—

running, it's spring

The haiku in this collection span from 1992 to the present, yet the impulses behind Kamakura's work stem, in part, from a year she spent in Paris with her husband, the poet Ban'ya Natsuishi, in the late 1990's. According to Kamakura, during her travels in Europe, her sense of the possibilities for haiku expanded and she began to compose poems more freely.

This freedom can be found throughout her work, which often relies on natural phenomena to freight her emotional life. Sunlight. Water. Wind. Sky. These are some of the elements that constitute the raw material of her poems, but they are never static:

ベランダの光は風の上で休む

beranda no hikari wa kaze no ue de yasumu

Rays of sunlight

from the porch

rest on the wind

The sunlight does not "seem" to rest, but rather, it simply rests; the force of her imagination compels the reader to believe in the scene, the rays of sunlight as something alive, the actuality of two intangible elements—wind and light—touching each other.

And consider the ways in which she speaks for everyday objects with a generous sympathy:

この暑さ定規は目盛り捨てたいよ
kono atsusa jougi wa memori sutetai yo

This summer heat—

the ruler wants

to remove its gradations!

Keen, compassionate and funny, the poem animates the critical details that make up the world. At the same time, there's also a more serious, even mysterious, tone to some of her poems:

神あるいは日輪という寒き円
kami aruiwa nichirin toiu samuki en

A cold circle

called God

or the sun

This haiku invites a marvelous resolution on its own terms: the paradoxical surface—God as a circle, a cold sun—may be seen as the indifferent cycles of nature, the sun shining in winter. The juxtaposition of complex images with accessible language serves as a key feature of Kamakura's work, an element that both challenges and welcomes us.

James Shea

Chicago, 2007

序文

アメリカの詩人であるジェームス・ライトは、かつてロバート・フロストの「打ち込んだ」という短い詩の中で「実際に」という言葉のもつ力を例にあげ、「一つの副詞が弾丸となって私の心を打つ」と言った。特に俳句は、それぞれの言葉が大変なプレッシャーをかけあう。鎌倉佐弓の俳句では、主に一つの単語が一行全体に反響している。次の「しがみつく」という動詞、あるいは「cling」のように。

夏の果スポンジに水しがみつく

Natsu no hate suponji ni mizu shigamitsuku

The end of summer—

water clings

to a sponge

さらに、鎌倉は嬉しいエネルギーの炸裂を表すセンスを持つ。二つの音節だけで読者を驚かせるような才能をみせる。

ポストまで歩けば二分走れば春

posuto made arukeba nibun hashireba haru

Walking, it's two minutes

to the mailbox—

running, it's spring

この句集は１９９２年から現在までの期間がかかっている。しかし、９０年代後半、一年間、夫の俳人夏石番矢と一緒にパリに住んだ経験が鎌倉の発想センスの広がりにいっそう拍車をかけた。鎌倉によると、ヨーロッパを旅行中、俳句を詠む可能性の感覚が豊かになり、より自由に詩を作り始めたそうである。

この自由さは彼女の感情的な人生を表現するためによく自然現象を
つかう句の中に、見つけることができる。光、水、風、空。これら
は鎌倉の句の原材料としての要素のいくつかであろうが、決して静
的なものではない。

ベランダの光は風の上で休む

beranda no hikari wa kaze no ue de yasumu

Rays of sunlight

from the porch

rest on the wind

光は休むようなものではなく、むしろ、ただ単にそこにあるものだ
。彼女の想像力は、読者に、生きているものとしての光線を感じさ
せ、二つの形がないエレメント–風と光–が、互いに触れあっている
と信じさせようとする。

さらに、気前のよい共感で日常の物に語りかけている様子をみてみ
よう：

この暑さ定規は目盛り捨てたいよ

kono atsusa jougi wa memori sutetai yo

This summer heat—

the ruler wants

to remove its gradations!

この句は鋭く情が深い一方で、滑稽さもそなわり、世界を構築して
いる重要な細部に生命を吹き込んでいる。が、同時に、より真剣で
さらに神秘的なトーンの入っている句もある。

神あるいは日輪という寒き円

kami aruiwa nichirin toiu samuki en

A cold circle

called God

or the sun

一句の中で素晴らしい解決をみせている。逆説的な表面–円のよう
な神、寒い太陽–無関心な自然のサイクル、冬の太陽が輝くとして
みら

れるだろう。分かりやすい言語と複雑なイメージが並列することが
、鎌倉の作品に関する重要な特色で、ともに私たちを刺激し、さら
に次の俳句を歓迎する要素となっている。

ジェームス・シエイ

シカゴ・２００７年

1　返事はハミングで

1 Reply by Humming

ほほえみは雲より軽しスイートピー

Our smiles

lighter than a cloud—

sweet peas in bloom

地平線うさぎは透きとおって越す

Transparent—

a rabbit

crosses the horizon

巴里を映す水晶体の青からん

Reflecting Paris,

my crystalline lens

must be pure blue

「暖かいね」わたしの返事はハミングで

"Isn't it warm?"

I reply

by humming

万華鏡いちばん奥に王の部屋

In the deepest part

of the kaleidoscope:

the Emperor's room

風船と甲板と白日の五月

A balloon,

a deck of a ship,

and a bright sun in May

はるかなる石の王妃へ薔薇かんむり

For the stone Queen

far in the distance:

a crown of roses

ギリシアのアの音ひびく雨あがり

The echoing sound

of the Greek letter "alpha"—

the rain stopping

ポストまで歩けば二分走れば春

Walking, it's two minutes

to the mailbox—

running, it's spring

にんじんの欠伸は泥がついている

The yawn of a carrot

is covered

with mud

君のそば桜草なら咲いていい

If I'm a primrose

at your side,

I'm allowed to bloom

伝えきく春の顔とは龍のかお

Tradition says

the face of Spring

is the face of the dragon

パセリひと呑み鍵かけて来たかしら

I swallowed

a piece of parsley—

Did I lock the door?

この暑さ定規は目盛り捨てたいよ

This summer heat—

the ruler wants

to remove its gradations!

まな板と猫と小指と日向ぼこ

A cutting board,

a cat and a pinky

basking in the sun

駅前が好きで噴水よく落ちる

Enjoying the station plaza—

sprays of water

fall from the fountain

風の背中にあたまに肩に鬼やんま

On the shoulder,
head and back of the wind:
dragonflies

向日葵をかかげ青空は止まらない

Hoisting up
a sunflower,
the blue sky never ends

2　渦巻く青

2 Whirling Blue

いちまいの布を乳房へ春の風

A piece of cloth

on the breasts—

the spring breeze

真っ先にあたまが濡れて木の芽時

First my head

gets wet

tree budding season

祭壇にすこしの蜜とあまたの冷え

A little nectar

and a deep chill

on the altar

ゆらゆらり樹のてっぺんはいつも空席

Always an open seat

at the top

of a swaying tree

山から人へ青色ときに渦を巻く

Blue from mountains

to humans, sometimes

it whirls

大空に請われるままに木の芽吹く

Just as the sky

requests—

the tree buds bloom

五月来よこの世のどこも汚さずに

Come, May!
Without soiling
our world!

空澄むや空の痛みは限りなし

The sky clears—
the sky's pain
has no limits

作品がすべて蒲公英は根がすべて

All of the poems

in the dandelions—

the roots are everything

われこそは大地であると蟇

"*I'm* the ground!"

thinks

the toad

蔦・杉・松ひかりが集う樹よいずこ

Ivies, cedars, pines:

Where is a tree

on which the light converges

野の岩のここには虹が帰ってくる

Back to the rock

in the field,

a rainbow returns here

昼下がり泉は水にいやされて

In early afternoon,

the fountain gets

healed by the water

天窓を壊すなら今　花ふぶけ

To break a skylight

right now:

Blow, cherry blossom storm!

草の絮きれいな空をさがしおり

Grass seeds

flying to discover

the pure sky

滅びてはならざるものへ春霞

A spring mist moves

toward the thing

that must not fall away

確かなのは好きということ風が好き

Certain

of the thing I like:

I like the wind

誰がための春ぞ大きく弧をえがく

For whom

is the spring?

Tracing a vast arc

3　夢は夢

3 A Dream Is a Dream

ハンカチ開く今日がきれいになるように

To make

the day clean,

I open a handkerchief

風は無形召しませ黄バラ赤いバラ

Wind has no shape—

please accept the yellow roses

and the red roses

いつ雲に追いこされしか雲まぶし

The blinding cloud—

when was I passed by it?

虹色のうろこを求め蛇泳ぐ

Searching for

rainbow-colored scales,

a snake swims

夜も回る水車会いたい人がいる

The waterwheel

turning even at night—

there's someone I'm eager to see

寝て起きて泥かきまぜて国造り

Sleeping, getting up,

and stirring mud—

making a country

倒れやすき菖蒲には水　君には酒

Water for an iris

that falls easily—

and wine for you

蛾のなきがら天与の塵とおもうべし

The moth's dead body:

consider it as dust

sent from heaven

蕗のとう小さくたって夢は夢

The butterbur stem:

even if small,

a dream is a dream

金輪際大地となりぬ　なりたかったか

Certainly

you have become the earth—

Did you want to be?

水を渡り山越えるべし希望まで

We shall cross the water

and pass the mountains

until we reach "hope"

空見る自由つぶれる自由　蟻に

Freedom to watch the sky

freedom to be trampled

for an ant

我は汝を想う星は星をおもうや

I care about you—
does a star
care about a star?

ちぎれ雲ときにはこの指に止まれ

Patch of clouds—
someday
perch on this finger!

夏終る引き出しに雲入れたまま

The summer ends—

pulled out clouds

put back just as they are

<ruby>横断歩道<rt>ゼブラゾーン</rt></ruby>わたしの風を待っている

A zebra crossing—

I'm waiting

for my wind

4　われらの声

4 Our Voices

朝始まる群青色の糸切れて

The morning begins—

a deep blue thread

breaks

はためいてシーツから詩の湧くところ

At the same moment

a new poem springs

out of a fluttering sheet

星をあきらめクローゼットに服いっぱい

Giving up the stars,

my closet

full of dresses

家捨てる子蜘蛛らにうす青き糸

Pale blue threads

from each baby spider

escaping from their home

砂が手にくっつく眠たくてならぬ

Sand clinging to

my hands

I'm terribly sleepy

ほの暗きことが大事な玉手箱

A dimness

is a precious

treasure chest

天国の門はとおくて花満開

The gates of paradise

are so distant—

cherry blossoms in full bloom

猫を屋根に月をひがしに我が夫

A cat on the roof,

the moon in the east,

my husband

太陽へ父に似た子が走りだす

A child resembling

her father starts to race

toward the sun

冥界の母をねむらす桐一葉

A fallen paulownia leaf

puts my mother to sleep

in the afterlife

五、六、七、もちろん八も暖かい

Five, six, seven

and of course

eight is also warm

天を指す人差し指が霧の中

Fog—

my index finger

pointing to the sky

地団駄を踏んでも斧は沼の底

Even stamping my feet

on the ground—

the axe was at the bottom of the marsh

膝曲げて眠るよ父と子と胡瓜

They bend their knees

in sleep: the father,

child, and cucumber

母は泉こころおきなく水飲んで

The mother is a spring—

drinking water

to her heart's content

夏の果スポンジに水しがみつく

The end of summer—

water clings

to a sponge

赤黄黒どれも見果てぬ空のいろ

The colors of the sky

are never

red, yellow or black

われらの声明るくあれようろこ雲

Let our voices

be delightful!

Mackerel clouds

5　海はラララ

5 La La La the Sea

ぎしと鳴る冬の夕陽に近づくな

Don't get any closer

to the creaking

winter sunset!

夕茜まばゆいときの海はラララ

Evening glow:

la la la the sea

dazzling

秋水の裏はなやぐと覗き込む

The bottom of the autumn water—

Peeking in to find it

happy

おろかにも日矢を楽しむ浮こおり

Stupidly,

the floating ice

enjoys the rays of sun

辿りつけぬどんなに薔薇を抱えても

I cannot get there—

even though

I carry these roses

風夕べ石榴を割ってまださまよう

After breaking a pomegranate,

an evening wind

still wanders about

蓑虫の内なる光屈めるや

Inside the cocoon

of the bagworm—

perhaps sunlight bends

睫というあえかな繁み小鳥くる

Little birds come

to a delicate bush

called "eyelashes"

神あるいは日輪という寒き円

A cold circle

called God

or the sun

冬銀河から「お帰り」という声が

From the wintry Milky Way

a voice says:

"Welcome Home!"

畏れとは紅葉の色に似ているや

Our fear

may resemble the colors

of autumn leaves

その昔凍りついたる樫おもえ

Can you remember

that frozen oak

from long ago?

月光の騎士には月光の従者

A knight in the

moonlight has

attendants in the moonlight

天も雪を見るらし雪の降りはじめ

The sky also seems

to see the snow—

first snowfall

芒原さんざん枯れているもよし

So lovely

a field of Japanese pampas grass

completely withered

われに棲む馬鹿と阿呆と夕あかり

Residing in myself:

a fool, an idiot,

and an evening light

後半生冬のかすみに放ちおく

Set free the second half

of my life

in the winter mist

6　樹の間の永遠

6 Eternity Among the Trees

まだ夢はあるか　きつつき木を覗く

Do you still have dreams?

A woodpecker peeps

through a tree hole

永遠が見えそう枯木立ゆけば

If you walk

among the bare trees,

you can see eternity

ベランダの光は風の上で休む

Rays of sunlight

from the porch

rest on the wind

空き瓶を吾子の星出たり入ったり

My daughter's star
going in and out
of the empty bottle

飛べるかしら蓑虫じっと考える

I wonder if I can fly—

silently

the bagworm thinks hard

天守にてあふれる青と消えゆくあお

At the castle tower,

overflowing blue and

disappearing blue

枢には窓を海原には風を

For a coffin,

a window,

for the sea, the wind

舞う黒揚羽ビーナスはすでに裸身

A flittering black swallowtail—

Venus was already

a naked body

窓夕べ空があるから閉められる

There's an evening sky

in the window,

so it's closed

モナリザの遠景かぜが立ち去りぬ

From the background

of "Mona Lisa",

the wind has left

善悪いずれ雪原は雪ゆきゆき

Whether right or wrong,

the snowy field

fills with snow

残らぬ虹　日本語は残るだろうか

A rainbow

that won't remain—

will Japanese remain?

いつか膝きっとまばゆき雲まとう

Someday my knees

will be wrapped

in brilliant clouds

鎌倉　佐弓

1953年高知県生れ。埼玉大学在学中より俳句を作る。能村登四郎、林翔に師事。1988年沖珊瑚賞。叙情性豊かな作風で注目される。1998年より俳句雑誌「吟遊」を夏石番矢と刊行。編集にあたる。日本を始めスロヴェニア、ポルトガル、ブルガリアでの俳句や詩の国際的な集まりに参加、俳句を朗読する。2001年現代俳句協会賞。主な句集に『潤』（1984）、『水の十字架』(1987)、『天窓から』(1992)、『鎌倉佐弓句集』(1998)、『走れば春』(2001)、英訳句集『歌う青色』(2000)。著書に『現代俳句パノラマ』(1994)、『現代俳句ハンドブック』(1995)、『現代俳句集成
全一巻』(1996)など。その俳句は英語のほか、ギリシア語、ロシア語、ブルガリア語、ポルトガル語、韓国語などに翻訳されている。世界俳句協会会計。

Sayumi Kamakura

She was born in Kochi Prefecture, Japan, 1953. She began composing haiku while a student at Saitama University and studied haiku under the guidance of Toshiro Nomura and Sho Hayashi. In 1988, she won the Oki Sango Prize. The lyrical style of her haiku attracted attention, and in 1998 she established the haiku magazine "Ginyu" with Ban'ya Natsuishi, and has been its Editor since that time. She has attended international haiku or poetry festivals held in Japan, Slovenia, Portugal and Bulgaria. In 2001, she won the Modern Haiku Association Prize. Her published haiku collections include: *Jun* (*Moisture*, 1984), *Mizu no Jujika* (*Water Cross*, 1987), *Tenmado kara* (*From the Skylight*, 1992), *Kamakura Sayumi Kushu* (*Haiku of Sayumi Kamakura*, 1998). *Hashireba haru(Run to Spring, 2001),* She co-authored *Gendai Haiku Panorama* (1994), *Gendai Haiku Handbook* (1995), *Gendai Haiku Shusei Zen 1 Kan* (*Contemporary Haiku Anthology in One Volume*, 1996), etc. She also published, in both Japanese and English, *A Singing Blue: 50 Selected Haiku* (2000). Her haiku has been translated into English, Greek, Russian, Bulgarian, Portuguese and Korean. She is a member and Treasurer of the World Haiku Association.

www.ingramcontent.com/pod-product-compliance
Lightning Source LLC
Chambersburg PA
CBHW061259140726
47998CB00006B/2283